HEADstart

PANDAS

First published in Great Britain by
CAXTON EDITIONS
an imprint of
The Caxton Book Company,
16 Connaught Street,
Marble Arch, London, W2 2AF.

ISBN 1 84067 023 1

A copy of the CIP data for this book is available from the British Library upon request.

With grateful thanks to Helen Courtney

Created and produced for Caxton Editions by
FLAME TREE PUBLISHING,
a part of The Foundry Creative Media Company Ltd,
Crabtree Hall, Crabtree Lane,
Fulham, London, SW6 6TY.

Printed and bound in Singapore

HEADstart

PANDAS

KAREN SULLIVAN

Contents

What is a Panda?

The name 'panda' applies to two East Asian animals. Although they are considered to be relatives, the giant panda is sometimes classified as a bear, and the lesser panda, also known as the red panda, or common panda, is considered to be part of the racoon family.

The giant panda is one of the best-known animals in the world. It is larger than the common or lesser panda, and has a thick, woolly, white coat with black fur on the legs and ears. The animals are distinguished by black eye patches and a black band across the shoulders.

The lesser panda is found in China, Myanmar, Sikkim and Nepal in high mountain forests and bamboo thickets. Because of its unusual cat-like appearance, it is sometimes called a bear cat, or cat bear.

Pandas have lived in China for thousands of years, but they have always been rare. Today, the giant panda is one of the rarest animals in the world. There are only about 1,000 pandas in the whole of China, and less than 20 in zoos around the world. The World Wide Fund for Nature (WWF), which is the world's best-known conservation organization, has chosen the giant panda as its symbol.

The giant panda was highly valued by ancient Chinese emperors, partly because there were so few of them. In 1869, a French priest, Father Armand David, discovered the panda on his travels throughout China, and he wrote of 'a black and white bear', bringing home the skin and bones to be studied by scientists in Paris. The first living pandas were brought to the USA in 1936, and to London in 1938.

The Panda Family

The name panda refers to two separate species of mammal. The giant panda's scientific name is 'Ailuropoda melanoleuca', and it is part of the bear family: 'Ursidae'. The red panda's scientific name is 'Ailurus fulgens', and it is part of the racoon family: 'Procyonidae'.

The grouping of pandas has confused scientists for years. The Chinese called the panda the 'daxiongmau', which means 'large bear-cat', but this name can be misleading. The giant panda is actually related to bears, but although the panda looks like a bear, it does not have the same characteristics as other bears, such as black, brown and polar bears. It is also quite different from the racoon family, with which it is also grouped. Some experts believe that pandas belong to a separate family altogether, the 'Ailuridae', which is simply a 'panda family'.

One point that sets giant pandas apart from their bear cousins is the fact that although they are classified as a 'carnivore', a creature that preys on other animals, they differ from other carnivores because they do not eat meat. Other bears are 'omnivores', which means they will eat almost anything. Pandas are plant eaters, and they only feed on a single group of plants: the bamboos. This explains why many people call the panda a 'bamboo bear'.

The Giant Panda

One million years ago the giant panda lived in a wide area of China and what is now Myanmar. As the climate became drier and humans began to move into its habitat, the pandas gradually moved into the relatively small area of bamboo forest in the mountains on the edge of Tibet.

The giant panda has been the subject of Chinese literature and legend for many years. More than 1,000 years ago, a poet wrote that pandas had magical properties and that paintings of the panda could ward off evil spirits. People in the West did not know about pandas until 1869, and the first Westerners to shoot a giant panda were two sons of the American President Theodore Roosevelt: Theodore Junior and Kermit, in 1928.

Until the 1970s, very little was known about the giant panda's behaviour or biology. In 1975, an event occurred which encouraged a

great deal of research into the panda. In Northern Sichuan Province, in the heart of panda country, many of the bamboo plants began to die off. This meant that the pandas had nothing to eat, and around 150 giant pandas died of starvation. Chinese officials organized a 'census', an official count, which showed that there were only about 1,000 pandas remaining in China.

In 1980 the Chinese joined forces with the WWF and began a huge project to protect the giant panda. They set up conservation programmes and began to study the panda, in an attempt to prevent it from becoming extinct.

Characteristics of the Giant Panda

The giant panda lives in the cool, damp bamboo forests of central China. Its thick, woolly coat is black or brownish-black and yellowish-white. The darker colour forms patches around the ears, legs, and chest, and forms a band across the shoulders.

The giant panda is about 1.2 to 1.5 metres long (4 to 5 feet) from the tip of its nose to its rump, and it has a stubby tail. Adults weigh about 75 to 160 kilograms (165 to 350 pounds).

Pandas are solitary animals, and they prefer to be on their own. Against the dense green vegetation of their natural habitat they can spot each other from a distance, and avoid coming into contact. While on the

ground a panda is easy to spot, but once it climbs a tree, the black of its coat is camouflaged against the bark and the white fur is hidden by the light of the sky shining through the branches. This means that the panda can hide from predators when it senses danger.

Pandas have very sensitive hearing and a sharp sense of smell, but their eyesight is not good. They walk clumsily with a flat-footed waddle while on the ground, but they are agile climbers and sometimes sleep in the trees. They enjoy splashing in water, but they do not swim.

Pandas can live as long as 30 years. Males and females are similar in appearance, except that females are slightly smaller. The thick, waterproof coat protects it from the cold and damp. The short shaggy tail protects the scent glands. It is also used as a brush to paint the panda's scent when it wants to make its mark. All pandas have powerful claws which they use to grip trees.

Natural Habitats of the Giant Panda

The giant panda, a rare and closely protected animal, lives in the cool, damp bamboo forests of mountainous central China, generally at heights of 1,500 to 4,000 m (5,000 to 13,000 ft). At one time the panda population was much more widespread, but today it is found only in remote and unspoiled areas of land, where there are few roads or signs of human life.

The mountains where they live are covered with forests of edible bamboo. It is so dense in parts that it is impossible to see more than a few metres, but this is not important to the panda, which does not have good eyesight. The forests have thick undergrowth, and most pandas tunnel through this, so that they can move silently and quickly across the land, while remaining concealed.

The panda's habitat has many streams, rivers and spectacular waterfalls. The panda requires a great deal to drink, so it is important that it has a good supply of water to survive. The mountain forests are cold, and it often snows, but their coats provide them with the necessary warmth. Pandas are mainly ground dwellers, using caves, hollow trees, or rock crevices for shelter, but they will climb trees to escape danger, or perhaps to sleep.

What Giant Pandas Eat

Bamboo is the main diet of the panda, although it may nibble at other plants from time to time. On some occasions, it may even swallow a small animal, such as a bamboo rat, but normally it feeds exclusively on the stems, twigs, leaves and fresh young shoots of various types of bamboo. Sometimes pandas catch small fish. Experts believe that pandas would have a diet of meat if they were able to prey on other animals, but because they are bad hunters and are far too heavy to chase other animals, their diet is mainly vegetarian.

The panda prefers a type of bamboo, called 'chinacane', which is much like sugar cane. They eat the leaves and the young shoots as well as the juicy pith inside the stems.

Bamboo, like grass, is very difficult to digest, and many animals, such as cows, have special digestive systems that allow them to cope, including more than one stomach and very long intestines. The panda, however, has one stomach and very short intestines, which means that digesting the bamboo is difficult. This means that in order to get enough nourishment from the bamboo, the panda must eat between 10 and 20 kilograms of it a day (between 22 and 45 pounds). Pandas feed for roughly 14 hours a day, in order to consume these quantities.

Because they do not need to hunt for their food, and because it is readily available all year round, the giant panda does not need to hibernate, or to store food for the winter. There are almost no other animals which compete for food in the mountains, so pandas can remain in their habitat all year round without worrying about finding something to eat.

Pandas sit upright with their backs propped against trees in order to eat. They bite off a length of bamboo and use their forepaws to hold the food to their mouths. They strip off the tough outer part of the cane, and then crush the pith with large, strong jaws and teeth. Both the giant and red pandas have a type of thumb, called a 'pseudo thumb', which allows them to grip the bamboo. In fact this is not a thumb at all, but an enlargement of the wristbone, covered by a leathery pad. This 'thumb' makes the panda's forepaws more mobile and able to perform precise movements.

In order to help the digestive process, pandas drink huge quantities of water from mountain streams and rivers. There are many local legends about how much a panda can drink. Tibetan legend suggests that pandas drink so much water that they become 'drunk'. When the snows melt in

early spring, pandas come down the mountains in search of water. It is believed that when they see their reflections in the water, they think they are seeing another panda, and quickly drink as much water as they can, to prevent the 'other panda' from having it. Pandas can, it seems, drink until they are unable to move, and will collapse on the ground to sleep off the effects of having drunk so much.

Pandas spend roughly two-thirds of their day feeding, and the remainder of their time is spent sleeping or resting. Pandas have no particular sleeping place, but lie on the ground wherever they happen to be: day or night. Feeding occurs in stretches of three to four hours, after which the panda will simply flop down and relax.

The Life-Cycle of the Giant Panda

Pandas live in 'territories' that are about two to three kilometres in diameter. Normally a panda will spend its whole life there, although sometimes it may move on, or accept a new panda into its territory quite gracefully.

Pandas eventually mate in order to have babies or 'cubs'. They begin to have young when they are about six years old. During the short breeding season in the spring (usually from March to May), a female panda which is ready to mate leaves a message for a male panda by 'painting' her scent on to rocks and plants with her tail. The female panda may also make quite loud noises, something like the bleat of a lamb, to attract attention. Male pandas will find the female based on her scent messages, and on her cries. Female pandas choose one mate every year, and will drive away any other males that come calling.

The female usually needs time to become accustomed to a strange male, as pandas normally have a different partner each year. Males often show off to try to impress the female. They may roar and bark, or climb trees and perform acrobatics. In many cases, a male has to wait a long time for the female to accept him, but mating eventually takes place.

Male pandas do not have paternal, or 'fatherly', feelings, and are not interested in their offspring. Female pandas are pregnant for about five months, and most panda cubs are born in September. Pandas give birth in the safety of a cave or a hollow tree to one or, occasionally, two cubs. Panda twins are less common, and the second-born usually dies.

Pandas weigh about 100 grams (about a quarter of a pound) when they are born, and they are about 15 cm (7 ins) long. They are pink, with white fur, and rely completely on their mothers.

The cubs do not have teeth, and they are

as helpless as new-born babies. A panda mother will hold her cub for the first few weeks of life, never letting it go. She holds it against her breast, and licks it to keep it clean.

Panda cubs grow quickly, and by one month old they will have the characteristic black and white patterns. The black eye patches appear as early as the sixth day after birth, followed by the ear and shoulder markings and finally the legs will darken. A panda cub starts to crawl at about three months old, and it will be able to move around without help from its mother by the age of four months.

The mothers teach their cubs everything they need to know about survival, including protecting themselves from other animals, eating, drinking, and leaving scent messages for other pandas. A panda is able to look after itself by the age of six months, but will stay with its mother until it is about a year and a half old. At this time, it goes in search of its own territory.

A panda is fully grown at four years, and at the age of five or six, it will begin looking for its own mate, to start a family. Pandas raise only one cub every two years in the wild.

Pandas can live for up to 20 years, but many pandas die long before this – one of the reasons why they are an endangered species.

Pandas at Risk

Pandas have never been common, partly because they produce very few young, and partly because they can only live in bamboo forests. Each panda requires a large area of forest to itself, so even a big stretch of land may be home to only a few pandas.

Their main diet, bamboo, is not always a reliable source of food. For up to a hundred years the bamboo plants will spread and grow. Suddenly, and usually without warning, they will flower, make seeds and then die, leaving no food for the pandas until the new plants grow. Some bamboo plants flower every 20 to 30 years, which can be particularly dangerous for pandas.

In the past, pandas would have been able to travel to new territories, where food was still plentiful, but today they are confined to the mountain ranges, and cannot travel down into the valleys, or across to other ranges, because of the human settlements and cultivated land in between.

Bamboo forests are also becoming smaller and fewer as the population of China grows. More land is now required for farms, rice fields and villages, and forests are being cut down to accommodate the number of people on the land, and to provide timber for their houses.

Pandas have also become endangered through hunting, which carried on despite a ban that was put in place in 1962. In the past, pandas were captured to take to zoos around the world, but this is no longer allowed and the government only lets a certain number of pandas go to zoos in different countries where they will be cared for properly. However, pandas are still killed for their skins, which are often used as sleeping mats and rugs. Panda skins are also believed to ward off evil spirits, and in some cultures, people will pay a great deal of money for a skin.

Today, pandas are considered to be 'national treasures', and are strictly protected by the Chinese government. Twelve panda sanctuaries or reserves have already been created to protect large stretches of panda territory, and to provide living space for up to 600 pandas.

The Chinese and American governments have set up a conservation programme, studying the panda in order to help it to survive. Local people also build feeding places for the pandas, putting large quantities of food out during times of bamboo 'die-back'. Rescue teams search the forests for weak or sick animals, which are cared for, fed and then released into territories where food is plentiful. Many volunteers have helped to ease the problem by planting large areas with bamboo. The inhabitants of 5,000 villages in Sichuan are also taught about the need to protect pandas, and how to care for starving pandas. They have now learned the importance of maintaining bamboo forests.

Breeding and Breeding Centres

The Chinese people have set up panda reserves and breeding centres, attempting to learn more about their national treasures in order to preserve them. It has proved very difficult to breed pandas in captivity, as they do not often mate if they are not in a wild environment.

The breeding centres now use a form of 'artificial insemination', which means that scientists collect sperm from a fully-grown male panda and freeze it in a tube. They can send the tube from one centre to another, or between zoos, and put the sperm into a female panda who is ready to mate. Many pandas have been born in breeding centres and zoos as a result of artificial insemination.

Zoos around the world share information about the pandas, in the race to learn enough about them to prevent their extinction. The panda 'stud-book', kept at the London Zoo, records all the important details of zoo pandas around the world, and helps zoo staff to plan future breeding.

Zoos have proved to be a good way to prevent the panda's extinction. They offer pandas a safe home, while helping them to breed. Pandas in zoos are kept in comfortable enclosures, with areas of grass and hard ground. Tree trunks are provided, and a pool in which they can bathe. Pandas also require a private den, and rocks and logs on which to leave their scent messages. Pandas are usually given fresh bamboo, along with other food that is easier to buy.

For a zoo to be permitted to keep pandas, it must agree to help others to breed them. Zoos often lend pandas for breeding. For example, in the 1960s, Chi-Chi, from the London Zoo was brought together with

An-An from the Moscow Zoo, in the hope that they would mate. Although this didn't work, later attempts to breed pandas naturally have been successful. In 1988, Chia-Chia, from the London Zoo, was taken to the Mexico City Zoo, where he mated successfully with many females. Unfortunately, panda cubs born in zoos usually die young, and it has not been possible to raise a young cub if its mother cannot look after it.

Panda reserves have also been created in China to protect the pandas and their bamboo forests. Armed guards patrol the reserves to protect the pandas from hunters, and to ensure that the local villagers do not destroy the trees. The largest reserve, at Wolong, was created in 1975. In 1980, the Chinese government and the WWF built a special panda-breeding and research centre there. Pandas are moved to these 'safe' areas, where plenty of bamboo grows to keep them healthy.

The panda is now seen as a symbol of China's determination to treat its wildlife and natural resources with respect, and the government is very involved in setting up conservation areas and in funding breeding centres and research.

The Red Panda

The red, or lesser, panda is found in the forested mountains of the Himalayas and western China at heights of 1,800 to 4,000 m (6,000 to 13,000 ft). Unlike the giant panda, the red panda lives in countries outside China, including Myanmar, Sikkim and Nepal.

It has a long, dense, woolly coat of reddish brown fur, with lighter coloured bands on the tail and dark red-brown or black undersides. Its face is white, with a reddish-brown stripe extending

down from each eye to the lower jaw. The red panda grows to 112 cm (44 ins) long, including a 48 cm (19 inch) tail, and weighs up to 5 kg (11 pounds).

The lesser pandas travel in pairs or small family groups. During the day this panda sleeps curled up in a tree with its tail over its head or sitting on a limb with its head tucked under its chest and between its forelegs. It feeds at night, eating bamboo sprouts, grasses, fruits, other plant material, and, occasionally, small animals. One or two young are born in the spring. They stay with the mother for about a year, or until the next litter is about to be born.

The red panda was discovered in 1825, and it is largely considered to be a close relative of the giant black and white panda, although they do not look very much alike. They both come from the same part of the world, eat similar food and both have special front paws which they use to hold food. However, red pandas are much more like racoons in appearance and behaviour, and they are 'nocturnal', prefering to come out at night and sleep during the day. For 50 years after its discovery, the red panda was thought to be the only panda to exist. It is slightly less rare than the giant panda, and can usually be found alongside its larger cousin on the reserves in China.

Panda Facts

Pandas are aggressively solitary animals, except during March and April when the females are ready for mating and allow males to approach them.

The giant panda occupies territories of about 2 square kilometres on average. In winter they range more widely, having to move to lower altitudes in search of unfrozen streams from which to drink.

A number of pandas have been 'tagged' with radio transmitters fixed to collars around their necks. The signals that are given off from these mean that researchers can plot the animals' movements on a map, and also to tell when they are active and resting.

Adult pandas have almost no predators, although young pandas are sometimes taken by leopards and wild dogs.

In recent years, the biggest threat to the giant panda's existence has been the natural disappearance of several species of bamboo rather than the activities of humans.

The panda has become the world's most expensive endangered species. The WWF has contributed more than two million pounds to giant panda conservation since 1980. It seems that despite the efforts of the government and conservation groups, there has not been an increase in the number of pandas in the wild. In fact, there may even be fewer now than there were 20 years ago.

The panda is considered to be the best-loved and most familiar of the world's 1.8 million named species of animals.

Famous Giant Pandas

In Beijing Zoo on 9 September 1963, Ming-Ming became the first panda cub to be reared successfully in captivity.

Shao-Shao, a female panda in Madrid Zoo, was the first panda to become pregnant through artificial insemination. In 1982 she had a baby using the sperm of Chia-Chia, from the London Zoo, after her own mate died.

One of the most famous pandas born into captivity was Ron-Shun, born to Mei-Mei, in the Chengdu Zoo in China.

Chia-Chia, a male panda from the London Zoo, has been taken to Mexico City, where he has fathered several cubs with female pandas in captivity. On the way to Mexico, he stopped off at the Cincinnati Zoo, in the USA, to raise money to help other pandas.

Su-Lin, first of the very few giant pandas to be shown in the West, came to the United States as an infant in 1936 and was a popular attraction at the Brookfield Zoo, near Chicago, in the USA, until his death in 1938. In April 1972, the Chinese government sent two others, a male and a female, to the National Zoo in Washington DC.

Where are the Pandas Now?

Only 15 giant pandas have been born outside China: five in Washington National Zoo in the USA, and seven in Mexico City's Chapultepec Zoo. The other births were in Tokyo and Madrid. None of the American cubs survived more than four days, although four of the Mexican offspring are

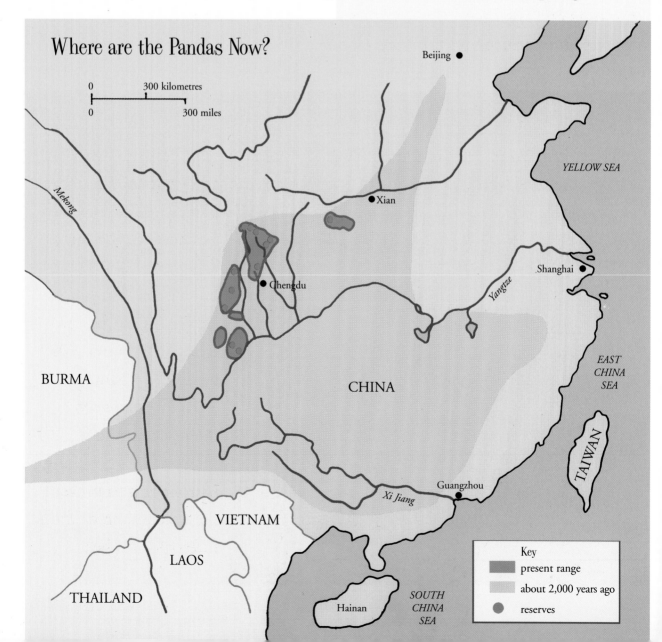

Where are the Pandas Now?

0   300 kilometres

0   300 miles

Beijing

YELLOW SEA

Mekong

Xian

Chengdu

Shanghai

Yangtze

BURMA

CHINA

EAST CHINA SEA

TAIWAN

VIETNAM

LAOS

Xi Jiang

Guangzhou

THAILAND

Hainan

SOUTH CHINA SEA

Key
present range
about 2,000 years ago
reserves

still alive. No one can think of a good reason why Mexico City should do better than zoos elsewhere, although it does happen to be at about the same altitude, or height, as the panda's natural habitat in western China. There have been births in Chinese zoos, but only one has been born so far in the breeding centre built at Wolong.

It seems that captive breeding is not the answer to the giant panda's survival. And the animal's prospects in the wild are not encouraging. It is confined to small isolated patches of natural habitat. The latest proposals by the WWF and its Chinese counterparts, include measures to increase the number

of panda reserves, which would mean that nearly half the 11,000 square kilometres of panda habitat would be protected; to maintain or re-establish bamboo 'corridors' between their patches; to improve anti-poaching patrols; and to prevent the destruction of the forests for timber.

Further Information

Places to Visit

The London Zoo – Regents Park, London, NW1 4RY. Telephone: 0171 722 3333
The Natural History Museum – Cromwell Road, London, SW7 5BD. Telephone: 0171 938 9123

Further Reading

BBC Wildlife magazine
British Wildlife magazine
Endangered Animals by Malcolm Penny, Wayland, 1988
The Fabulous Panda by M. de Havilland, Pan Books, 1987
The Giant Panda by Michael Bright, Franklin Watts, 1988
The Giant Panda by Ramona and Desmond Morris, Macmillan, 1981
Pandas by Christopher Catton, Christopher Helm, 1990
WWF News

Videos and CD Roms

Bears, Dorling Kindersley (video)
DK Children's Encyclopaedia, Dorling Kindersley (CD Rom)
A selection of videos on endangered species and other wildlife is available from the BBC and World Wide Fund for Nature.

Where to See Giant Pandas in Zoos

Washington DC, USA; Mexico City, Mexico; London, UK; Tokyo, Japan; Madrid, Spain; Paris, France; Toronto, Canada; Berlin, Germany; Chinese zoos.

Picture Credits